Barbara Gruber's *Ready Resource Books*

HOW TO USE WORD WALLS

How to Use Word Walls
Instant Word Wall Lessons & Activities for All Word Walls
by Barbara Gruber, M.A.

Contents

This book contains everything teachers need for successful word walls.

© Copyright 1999
All Rights Reserved
Printed in the USA
Practice & LearnRight
Publications
69992 Northhampton Ave.
Cathedral City, CA 92234

PLR3031
ISBN 1-58166-075-8

Practice & LearnRight

How to Use Word Walls
Instant Word Wall Lessons & Activities for All Word Walls
by Barbara Gruber, M.A.

Dear Teachers,

How can you use your word wall as a teaching tool?
This resource book is overflowing with ideas that will help you plan successful learning opportunities for children. It includes Instant Word Wall Lessons and Instant Word Wall Activities that engage students and teach skills. Your students will learn new words quickly. Your word wall will foster independence and help students master new words.

Do you already have a word wall that your students ignore?
This is an easy problem to solve! I'll show you how to have a word wall your students will use every day. This information-packed book provides busy teachers with proven, easy-to-implement ideas that work. Your word wall will be a teaching tool that coordinates with your reading and spelling programs. You and your students will use it daily throughout the year.

Are you ready to get a word wall up and running in your classroom?
This book will help you create a word wall that is educationally-sound. You can buy word walls or make your own! This valuable resource contains everything you need in one book for successful word walls without spending a lot of teacher time.

Keep this book handy -- it is packed with practical, creative ideas that work in classrooms everywhere with all reading programs!

Best wishes,
Barbara Gruber

Practice & LearnRight

Word Walls that Work !

How can you tell if a word wall is helping children learn words? Word walls work when students actually use them. You will see youngsters looking to the word wall for help with reading, spelling and figuring out how words work. It's as simple as that! If your word wall is being ignored by students, take it down and start over. You can put the same word wall up again. By using the ideas in this book, it will be a word wall that your students actually use! The classroom word wall can enhance your reading, writing and spelling programs. It can be a springboard for a wide variety of valuable learning activities! Consult this book for the ideas you need to get a successful word wall started today.

Perfect Places for Word Walls

A perfect place is where the word wall is easy to see from around the room. The word wall is a focal point in the classroom.

Pick a highly-visible spot for your word wall such as:

- a bulletin board -- cover the board with colorful paper or fabric.

- paper banners -- strung on a line.

- on the walls -- Is there space above the chalkboards or windows?

- the chalk board -- Will a section of your chalkboard work?

- across the windows -- Can you hang a big paper banner for words?

- a cardboard screen -- make a four-panel screen from a large appliance box. cover with paper or fabric.

Handy Hang-up Ideas for Word Cards

Hang cards so they can easily be moved around on the word wall. As you add words, you may need to move some of the word cards that are already posted. And, removable cards can be used for hands-on activities.

Ideas for posting cards:

On bulletin boards or cardboard screens, simply punch a hole in the top center of each card. Hang cards on pins. This is a quick way to hang cards and they are easy to move around!

On hard surfaces, use magnetic tape or velcro.

On chalkboards, use magnetic tape on the backs of the cards.
Double check to make sure your chalkboard is magnetic. Most chalkboards are!

Adhesive used on "stick-on notes" is now available as a glue. It comes in very handy in classrooms. It works well for posting word cards on paper back grounds.

If you use staples, tape or push pins and cards are not easily removed, make an extra set of cards for hands-on activities. One set goes on the word wall and the other set are in envelopes or on rings. An extra set of word cards that match the words on the word wall comes in handy for so many learning activities.

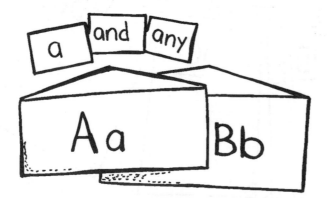

Practice & LearnRight

Systematic Word Walls

At some schools, teachers have standardized word lists used for word walls for each grade level. All students in first grade classrooms at the school, or in the school district, have the same words on their classroom word walls. The words increase in difficulty with each grade level. Teachers know the words the child learned the previous year. All students on grade level are exposed to the same words with this systematic approach. If you want to use a systematic approach to word walls, the word lists in this book can be used systematically.

A different approach for word walls is for teachers to select the word list they feel it is most important for their students to learn. Word walls help students with word skills -- that's what word walls are all about!

You'll want to do word wall lessons and activities every day throughout the year. It's a good idea to help parents understand the purpose of your word wall and how you use it at school. Point out the word wall to parents when they visit the classroom for meetings and conferences. Send home an informative letter about the classroom word wall. You may want to use the ready-to-go, reproducible letter on page 6. You may want to give parents a copy of the list of words that appear on your classroom word wall.

Practice & LearnRight

All About Our Classroom Word Wall!

Have you heard about our classroom word wall? If not, ask your child to tell you all about it. Word walls are word cards that are displayed on a classroom wall. It is important for your child to learn to read and spell our word wall words.

We do word wall activities every day to learn these important words. Ask your child to tell you about his favorite word wall activity. We do reading, writing, and spelling lessons with our word wall words.

You can help your child be a successful reader!

Read to your child. Continue to do this even after he/she can read independently. Reading together is the best way to help your child become a strong reader. Reading together helps your child develop a love for reading and learning. Establish a special time each day as "reading together" time.

When your child brings home schoolwork, look it over together. Ask your child to explain his/her schoolwork to you.

Help your child practice reading and spelling new words.
To make it fun, provide:

> crayons or washable felt pens for writing
> chalk and a chalkboard
> magnetic letters to spell words.

Showing an interest in your child's schoolwork let's your child know school is important. And, it shows that you value his/her efforts. The child who loves to read develops a lifelong desire to read and learn.

_____

Teacher/Date

Ready-to-Use Word Lists
Easy, High-Frequency Word Wall Words

Word List

a	done	here	me	she	who
all	down	him	more	side	why
also	each	his	most	so	yet
an	end	how	my	some	you
and	even	I	new	take	your
any	far	if	no	that	
are	feet	in	not	the	
as	find	into	now	thing	
at	for	is	of	this	
away	get	it	off	time	
be	give	its	old	to	
best	go	just	on	took	
big	got	kind	or	up	
but	had	let	out	us	
by	has	like	put	was	
can	have	look	same	way	
come	he	made	saw	we	
did	help	make	say	well	
do	her	may	see	will	

High-Frequency Word Wall Words

Word List

about	both	high	must	said	think	when
after	came	himself	need	second	those	where
again	could	knew	never	set	thought	which
almost	different	know	next	should	through	while
along	does	large	nothing	small	told	with
always	early	last	once	something	too	without
another	enough	later	only	still	toward	word
around	ever	left	open	such	under	work
back	every	little	other	than	until	would
because	few	long	our	their	use	young
been	first	many	over	them	very	
before	found	matter	own	then	want	
began	from	might	part	there	went	
better	good	more	point	these	were	
between	great	much	right	they	what	

Practice & **LearnRight**

Frequently Misspelled Word Wall Words

Word List

again	doctor	know	peace	school	too
already	does	instead	people	shoes	trouble
always	early	letter	piece	sometime	two
among	easy	little	please	soon	until
aunt	enough	loose	practice	store	used
because	everybody	many	pretty	straight	vacation
been	favorite	maybe	principal	suppose	very
before	first	minute	quarter	summer	weather
birthday	friend	morning	quit	sure	weigh
bought	getting	mother	quite	surprise	which
built	goes	nice	ready	terrible	whole
buy	guess	none	receive	thought	would
children	half	o'clock	remember	through	write
color	heard	off	right	tired	writing
could	hour	often	rough	together	your
country	house	once	said	tomorrow	
cousin	knew	party	Saturday	tonight	

Practice & LearnRight

Additional Word Lists That Make Sense for Word Walls

Children look to the word wall for help reading, writing and spelling words. Word walls are important teaching tools and references for students.

To use word walls effectively, use them for important words that children must learn to read and spell or difficult words and concepts. Easy-to-teach words and concepts such as synonyms, antonyms and theme words are handled more effectively with flash cards and vocabulary lists rather than word walls. Save your word walls for the kinds of words that are hardest for children to learn, such as:

High-frequency Words
Frequently-misspelled Words
You can outline word shapes to help children learn sight words.

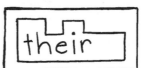

Word Families
Underline the rime (phonogram) in word family words.

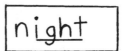

Contractions
Post cards side by side showing the contraction and the two words it stands for. Group cards under headers that show the word that the apostrophe is used for.

Homophones (words that sounds the same but are spelled differently). Post these words alphabetically. Show the word on the card with a phrase or sentence showing how it is used.

Prefixes and Suffixes
Post words alphabetically under header cards that show affixes.

Word Endings and Plurals
Post words under header cards for endings and plurals.

You can make word walls or buy Instant Word Walls as shown on inside back cover and back cover. Lists & Lessons for Teachers (PLR 3032) is packed with essential word lists and teaching activities. This handy book saves teachers time and work.

Word Cards That Work

Large, Same-size Word Cards Work Best!
Word Cards should be no smaller than 3" x 8".
Word cards should all be the same size.

Use Big Bold Letters!
Use big, bold print to write the words if you make your own word cards. Make one card and place it on the spot you have chosen for your word wall to make sure it is readable. If you buy a ready-to-go word wall, make sure the words are readable and the letters of the words are properly spaced.

Word Configurations
Outlining word shapes helps some students remember words. Outline word shapes for high-frequency words and frequently-misspelled words. Do not outline word configurations for word-families words.

Make sure the word shape around the letter "i" does not go as high as ascending letters. Make it go half as high as shown.

Making Header Cards
Words are posted in alphabetical order. You will need a header card for each letter of the alphabet. Make alphabet header cards in a different shape and/or color than the word cards on your word wall. Use large, bold print so header cards stand out and are easy to read.

Pages from shape notepads make colorful headers!

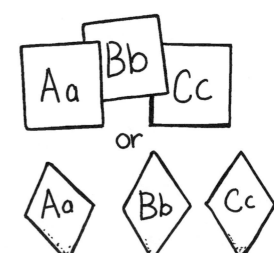

How to Create a Word Wall Students Use

Put words up gradually, instead of putting them up all at once. That's the secret to having a word wall children pay attention to! It's perfectly fine if it takes months until all the words are on the word wall. Focus on one or two words at a time. Whenever you add new words to your word wall do an Instant Word Wall Lesson shown on page 16. Post words gradually and use direct instruction to teach the words. After words are on the word wall, do Instant Word Wall Activities to provide practice and maintain word knowledge.

Link the word wall to as many areas of the curriculum as you can. Refer to the word wall during math, science and social studies lessons if there are words on the word wall that help students read and spell words they need. Help students make the connection that the word wall can help them with reading, writing and spelling in all subjects.

Routines are important in classrooms. They save valuable learning time and help teachers manage their classrooms successfully. Classrooms where predictable routines have been established foster responsibility and independence in children. Invest time in developing routines for introducing word wall words, such as the Instant Word Wall Lesson on page 16. There is another Instant Word Wall Lesson for Word Families on page 20. You may want to use these routines as described, modify them or develop your own. Once students become familiar with routines, lessons go quickly because children know what to expect and how to respond. You don't have to spend valuable time explaining what children should do. It is important to use the same procedure each time. Then you can expect your students to know exactly how to respond. When teachers vary from established routines, students often remind them how they "should be doing it." Routines can help you capitalize on the time you have to teach. When routines are established it is easier for teachers to teach and for children to learn. There should be many spontaneous happenings as well as predictable routines throughout the day in every classroom.

Practice & **LearnRight**

Word Wall Learning Time

Make word wall activities lively and fun with participation from every child. You may want to pick a certain time of day for word wall activities such as first thing in the morning, immediately following morning or just after lunch. Establishing a regular time makes it more likely that you will fit word wall activities into each busy learning day.

Ideas for working with your classroom word wall:

Ring wind chimes to capture childrens' attention when you are ready to work with the word wall. The pleasant sound catches everyone's attention and signals youngsters to focus on the word wall.

Jot a few word wall activities on the chalkboard. Tell students to choose an activity. Set a timer for five minutes to set a time period for students to do activities.

Word Wall Activities
Use crayons to write three words.
Build words with magnetic letters.
Read the word wall with a partner.

When you want to direct students' attention to specific words on the wall, use a colorful fly swatter or cobweb brush as attention-getting pointers!

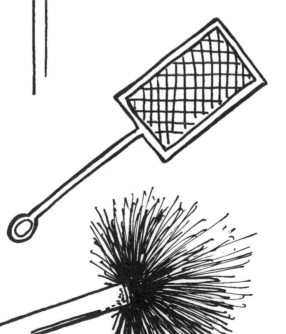

Jingles jazz up word wall lessons and activities. They are such fun for kids to hear, learn and say! Delight your class with special jingles for word wall activities. Challenge youngsters to help you create new jingles to use with the word wall. Jot the jingles on cards and put them on a ring. Or, write them on 9" x 12" oak tag cards. Children enjoy reading them and using them when they do word wall activities with partners or in groups.

Just for fun, give these jingles a try!

> One, two, three,
> Read with me!
> (or spell with me,
>   clap, tap...)

> Word wall, word wall,
> Read it now.
> Word wall, word wall,
> We know how!

> New words, new words,
> On the wall,
> We know we can,
> Read them all!

> Flashlight, flashlight,
> Oh so bright.
> Light the word wall,
> With your light!

> Let's spell it out!
> Please do not shout!

> Let's read, get ready, set, go,
> How many words do you know?

Motivate students to learn words with active learning. Have children write words on individual chalkboards, wipe-off boards or "magic slates." Buy a "doodle board" to use as a teaching tool. Write words on the "doodle board" when you are working with groups of children. Children can use it too! "Doodle boards" are sold in toy and variety stores. They come in a variety of sizes and shapes.

"g" is the second letter.

Doodle board

a _ _ _ n

Practice & LearnRight

14

Get Your Word Wall Going!

1. Use an Instant Word Wall that you have purchased or make your own word cards and headers. Take a look at the instant, ready-to-go word walls that are shown on the inside back cover and back cover. Arrange the word cards in order from the easiest to the most difficult word. You may want to group together certain word cards because it makes sense to introduce them together. For example, you may want to introduce the words an, and, and any at the same time.

2. Display the header cards on your word wall.

3. Introduce the first word for the word wall with an Instant Word Wall Lesson. The lesson is shown on page 16. Each time you add words, do an Instant Word Wall Lesson. When you use the same lesson each time, children know exactly what to do and the lesson can be done at a lively pace. It's a quick, high-interest way to present new words that involves 100% participation from every student. Use the Instant Word Wall Lesson shown on page 16 with any word list except word family words. A different lesson is provided for word family words on page 20.

After a few weeks, your word wall may look like this:

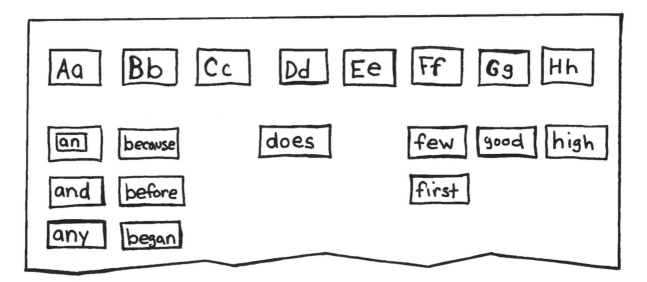

Eventually all the words will be on the word wall. Then, the word wall stays up as an important reference for children to use. Continue word wall activities to review words so children maintain word skills.

Instant Word Wall Lessons
Use for all Word Walls Except Word Families

Repeat this lesson for each new word you add to the word wall. Keep a snappy pace to make it interesting and fun. All students participate by spelling words aloud, reading aloud and visualizing new words.

1

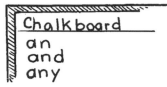

Write the word(s) on the chalkboard.
Point at one word and read aloud.
Say a sentence that uses the word.
Ask students to analyze the word(s).
Is it similar to a word on our word wall?
How are the words alike? Different?

2

Point at one word and read it aloud.
Have the class read the word aloud.

3

Point at the word again and spell it aloud.
Have the class spell the word aloud.

4

Now, have everyone close their eyes,
and picture the word in their minds.
Everyone spells the word aloud.
Point at the word and have everyone
read it aloud once again.

5

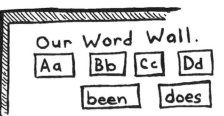

Post the word card on the word wall.
Point at the word and read it aloud
in unison one more time.

Practice & LearnRight

Word-Families Word Walls

On word families word walls, words are not displayed alphabetically. They are arranged by word families or grouped according to the vowel at the beginning of the rime. A few words about terminology: the words rime, spelling pattern, chunk and phonogram are used interchangeably. In the classroom, children confuse the words "rime" and "rhyme." It's easier for children to understand and remember terms such as "spelling pattern" or "chunk" instead of "rime."

Reading research* supports teaching common rimes. When children know the word "cat," they can use analogy to induce how to pronounce the word "sat." Focus on thirty-seven common rimes from which over five hundred words used in primary grades can be derived.

Thirty-seven Common Rimes for Word-families Word Walls

37 Basic Rimes

-ack	-eat	-ice	-ock	-uck
-ail	-ell	-ick	-oke	-ug
-ain	-est	-ide	-op	-ump
-ake		-ight	-ore	-unk
-ale		-ill	-ot	
-ame		-in		
-an		-ine		
-ank		-ing		
-ap		-ink		
-ash		-ip		
-at		-it		
-ate				
-aw				
-ay				

Adams, M.J. (1990). Beginning to read: Thinking and learning about print. Cambridge, MA: MIT Press.

Practice & LearnRight

Headers for Word-Families Word Walls

There are two effective ways you can display your word families word wall. Both approaches help children learn common rimes and give children opportunities to use analogy to figure out words. Take a look at the examples of these word walls and use the one you like best. They are both effective because they focus on the thirty-seven common rimes. An *Instant Word Wall Lesson for Word Families* is on page 20.

Vowels Header Cards
Your word families word wall can have header cards for the five vowels. Take a look at **Example A** below of this word wall. Just one word is displayed for each of the thirty-seven common rimes. Instead of teaching long and short vowels in isolation, vowel sounds are more stable when within a rime.

Thirty-seven Rimes Header Cards
You can have a header for each of the thirty-seven common rimes as shown in **Example B** on page 19. Post two or three words for each of the thirty-seven rimes. Children can use analogy to spell other words in the word families.

Example A: Word Families Word Wall Using Vowels as Headers

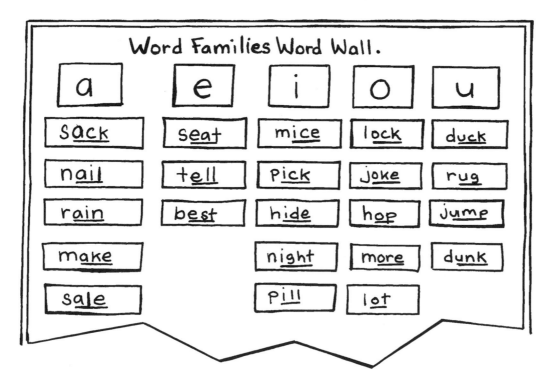

Practice & LearnRight

Example B: Word Families Word Wall Using 37 Rimes as Headers

-ack	-an	-aw	-ick	-ing	-op
back pack sack	can pan ran	jaw law saw	kick lick sick	king ring wing	hop pop

-ail	-ank	-ay	-ide	-ink	-ore
jail pail tail	bank sank tank	day say way	ride side wide	pink sink wink	more sore

-ain	-ap	-eat	-ight	-ip	-ot
gain pain rain	lap nap tap	heat seat meat	light night sight	hip lip	dot jot

-ake	-ash	-ell	-ill	-it	-uck
cake make take	cash dash mash	bell tell well	bill fill sill	bit sit	buck duck

-ale	-at	-est	-in	-ock	-ug
bale male sale	cat mat vat	best nest zest	bin pin win	dock lock	dug rug

-ame	-ate	-ice	-ine	-oke	-ump
came name same	date late mate	mice nice rice	fine line mine	joke woke	bump jump

					-unk
					dunk

Word Families Word Cards

For word family words, do not outline the configurations of the words. Instead, you can underline the letters in the rimes. We want students to focus on the common spelling patterns in words, not word shapes. Fluent readers do not decode words letter by letter-- they read words in chunks or spelling patterns.

Instant Word Wall Lesson for Word Families
Work on one family at a time.

1.

Write two or three words on the chalkboard
from the same word family.
Ask the class to analyze the words.
How are they alike? How are they different?

Yes - they do have the same spelling pattern. Let's underline it.

light
night

2.

It sounds the same. Look how it is spelled. Does it belong?

bite

bight

-ight
night
light
fight
bright
sight

Ask students to think of other
words in this word family.
As students call out words,
write them on the chalkboard.
Ask students if the word belongs?
Why does it belong?

3.

Let's read the -ight word family.

-ight
light
night
fight
bright
sight
might
right
tight

bite
kite
white
do not
belong

light

night

Read the list aloud together.
Then, choose one or two words from the
list to post on the word wall. Remind students posting all the words is unneces-
sary because if we can spell light, we
can figure out how to spell other words in
that word family.

Practice & LearnRight

Frequently Misspelled Word Wall Words

There are endless possibilities for learning opportunities using your word wall. Word Walls help children learn words and save teachers time and work. They are a source of ready-to-go activities that teach important word skills. The word wall is perfect as a springboard for so many individual, small group and whole class activities. The activities can provide practice on new words and review of all word wall words. Use the Word Wall Jingles on page 14 to add pizazz to learning word wall words.

Activities using your word wall can be:

- instantly usable with no teacher preparation time

- quick, fun-to-do with participation from every student

- for individuals, learning partners, small groups or the whole class

- done at childrens' desks, work stations or learning centers

- done orally, on individual chalkboards/write-on boards, or paper and pencil

- used with manipulatives such as magnetic letters or letter cards

- assigned or chosen by students

- used for homework assignments

- done during independent reading or reading workshop times

- perfect for transition times when children say "I'm done!"

You and your students will use the word wall so much, you'll wonder what you did without it. Take a look at the ready-to-go activities that work with all word walls on pages 22 to 47. And, get started today! There's a lot of learning going on when you are using your classroom word wall to teach word skills.

Instant Learning Activities for Word Walls

Rings of Word Cards with Sentences

Extend your word wall the easy way! Create a set of word cards that match the words on the word wall. Just cut a bunch of word cards from oak tag or cut sentence strips into word cards. Each time you add a word to the word wall, make a card and put it on a ring. Have a ring for each letter of the alphabet. Write a sentence on the card using the word. Rings of Word Cards work for so many activities that provide practice with word wall words. And when it comes to learning new words, children need practice, practice and more practice! Rereading words builds reading fluency!

Establish a place for your Rings of Word Cards. Challenge students to read the words and time themselves with a three-minute timer. Students love this activity on their own or with a learning partner.

Partners can take turns reading words.

Use a Clue

Stimulate youngsters to think with this learning activity. Place ten word cards along the chalk ledge or in a pocket chart. Use words that are already posted on the class-room word wall. Tell the class you want them to identify one of the words based on clues. After you give clues, have students tell you which words to remove. Through the process of elimination, children will be able to identify the word. Watch their eyes light up when they figure it out. For example:

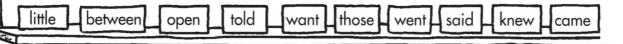

| little | between | open | told | want | those | went | said | knew | came |

Clues:
- the letter "e" is in the word
- each letter in the word is different
- the word has four letters
- the letter "n" is in the word
- the word can help you spell 'sent'

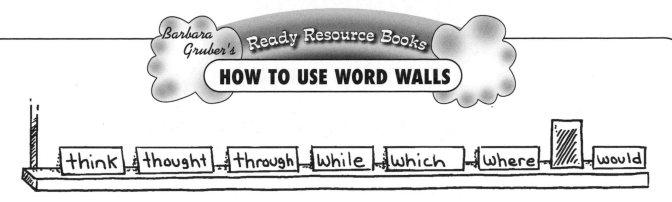

Turnover

Spread out ten word cards along the chalk ledge. Say a word and call on a student to go up and turn that card over. Continue to do this until all words are turned over.

Passout

Pass out a word card to every child. Say, if your word ends with "t" put it on the chalk ledge. After children have placed word cards on the chalkledge, read those words aloud with the class. Say, put your word card on the chalkledge if your word has three letters. Then read those words aloud with the class. Continue until all word cards are on the chalkledge and have been read aloud.

Play your favorite word card games using your word wall words.

Count, Clap and Read

Entertain your class with this group activity that gets everyone moving and reading words. It's called "Count, clap and read ." Have the class count aloud together: "One, two, three" Then have everyone clap three times in unison. Now, show a flash card and have the class read the word aloud. Count to three again, clap three times again, show another word card for the class to read. This is a perfect activity to do as children are entering the room until everyone is seated, or when you students are waiting in line.

Practice & LearnRight

Let's Read Our Word Wall Activities

Binnoculars
Just for fun, students can use binnoculars (made from toilet tissue tubes) or telescopes (paper towel tubes) when they read the word wall words.

Start the Day
Why not start every day by reading aloud the word wall with your class. It just takes a few minutes and is a terrific way to review all the words on the word wall.

Flashlight
Turn out the lights and close the drapes. Shine a flashlight on the words you want the class to read aloud.

Flashlight, flashlight, Oh so bright, Light the Word Wall with your light.

A-Z
Read the word wall from a to z aloud. Or, read it from z to a.

Sentence Strips
When you add a word to the word wall, write a sentence using that word on a sentence strip. Underline the new word in the sentence. Place the sentence strips in a pocket chart on along the chalkledge for rereading. When all the words are posted on your word wall, you will have a sentence strip for each word. All the sentence strips can be stored in a box or plastic wallpaper tray available at home improvement stores. Sentence strips can also be used at a reading center or in the classroom library. The sentence strips can be used by individual students, small groups or by the whole class.

I <u>thought</u> you were going home.

Goldilocks ran <u>through</u> the forest.

<u>Where</u> do you live?

Practice & **LearnRight**

Mascot

If you don't already have a cute stuffed animal as a class mascot, hurry up and get one! Have your class mascot hold a sign showing the newest word on the word wall.

Missing Words

Remove three words from the word wall when students are not in the room. Tell them three words are missing and ask if they can remember what they are? Give clues until the words are figured out. Clues can be the number of letters that are in the words, or the beginning letters of the missing words. After the class figures out which words are missing, place the word cards back on the word wall.

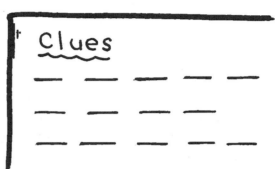

Stand Up & Sit Down

When the class has "the wiggles" get this activity going. It's called "Stand-up and sit-down reading." Students stand beside their chairs and read the first five words aloud together. Then they quickly sit down and read the next five words aloud. Then they stand for reading the next five words. They continue to stand and sit as they read all the words.

Name Words in Sentence

Before saying a sentence, ask the class to listen for words in the sentence that are on the word wall. Say the sentence and ask students to name the word wall words they heard.

Practice & **LearnRight**

VIP Visit

Capture kids' attention with a visit from someone special. Invite a very important person in to read the word wall with your class. Issue a special invitation to the principal, librarian or other staff member to come to your classroom to lead the reading of the word wall.

Ms Lee
Principal

Applause

Applause -- everyone loves to hear it! After you read the entire word wall aloud with your class, give yourselves a hand. Have the class applaud for ten seconds. Or recite one of the word wall jingles, on page 14, aloud together and then give a round of applause. Celebrate the learning that's going on!

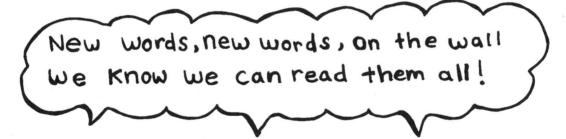

New words, new words, on the wall
We know we can read them all!

Lonely Letters

After you have all the words from your word list on your classroom word wall, you may have some letters of the alphabet that have no words. Have children suggest words for these letters. When you have a few suggestions, have the class decide which words they want to add to the word wall for the "lonely letters."

zoo   x-ray

zip

zipper

Get Your Word Wall Going!

Speedy Reader Challenge

After you have all word wall words posted, start the speedy reader program. If you have 100 words on your word wall, write the first 10 words on a 9 x 12 card cut from tagboard. Write the next ten words on another card so you end up with a set of ten cards. Number the cards from one to ten. Tell the class they can practice reading the word cards and they can let you know when they are ready to be a speedy reader. Keep track of students progress on a class list. When a student reads the words on the card aloud quickly and correctly, he can be checked off on that card. When students are checked off on all ten cards, give them well-deserved award certificates to take home. Ready-to-reproduce awards are on page 44.

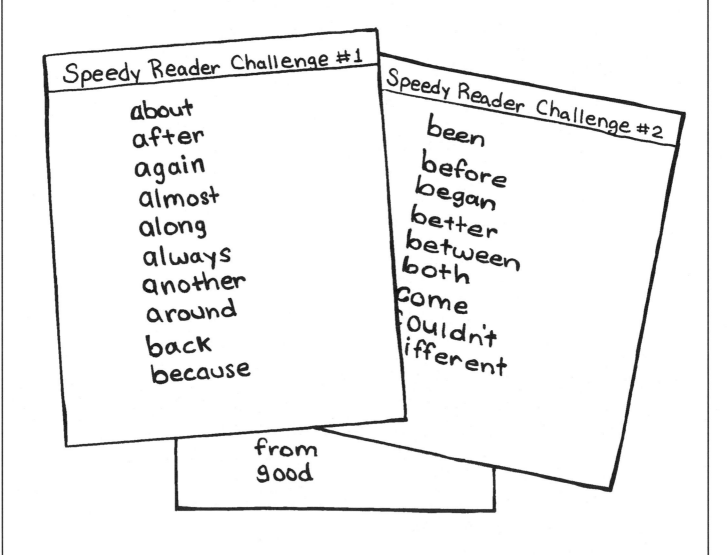

Speedy Reader Challenge #1

about
after
again
almost
along
always
another
around
back
because

Speedy Reader Challenge #2

been
before
began
better
between
both
come
couldn't
different

from
good

Let's Write Activities for Word Wall Words
Stimulate your students with high-interest writing activities.

Cut a basketful of 1" x 3" slips of construction paper to use as mini word cards. These blank mini word cards will come in handy!

Every student can have a desktop word wall. All it takes is an envelope for each child and blank mini word cards. When you add words to the classroom word wall, children write the same words on mini word cards and add them to their envelopes. The mini word cards in the envelope match the classroom word wall. Children can spread the little word cards out and make desktop word walls.
They can:

• Arrange the word cards in abc order. Read the words.

• Arrange words from the easiest to most difficult word. Read the words.

• Sort the words according to word length.

• Students spread out word cards and follow directions from the teacher such as:
  -touch the word 'little'
  -turn over the word 'that'
  -pick up the word 'book' and place it on top of a rhyming word
  -hold up the word that rhymes with 'peach'
  -touch the missing word in this sentence,
    "I need my umbrella (clap) it is raining.
  -put the word card in the envelope when I say the word:
    (call out words one by one for students to find and put away)

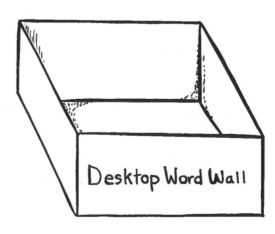

Desktop Word Wall

Keep envelopes in a box or basket filed in abc order, filed by first names.

Practice & **LearnRight**

Most Difficult Words

Have children look at the word wall. Ask each child to find three words that are most difficult for him/her to learn to spell. Children write the words on mini word cards and staple them into a little pocket-size study book. At the end of the day, students can take pocket study books home.

Newspaper Pairs

Give pairs of children a page from the newspaper. Tell students to use yellow crayons to highlight word wall words they find on the newspaper page. Set a timer. See how many word wall words the pairs of students can find in three minutes. Now that you've done this activity in the classroom, ask children to do it for "homework" tonight.

1-3-5-7

Call this activity 1-3-5-7! Using words from the word wall, children write one word with one letter, a word with three letters, a word with five letters and seven letters.

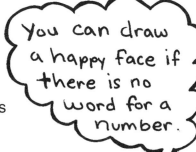

2-4-6-8

2-4-6-8 is the name of this activity. Everyone writes one word with two letters, a word with four letters, a six-letter word and a word with eight letters.

Bingo Blackout

Play a game to make learning words fun. Play "Bingo Blackout" with your class. Have children fold a piece of paper in half four times and then unfold it. The paper will be "divided" by folds into sixteen sections. Paper that is 16" x 20" works well for this. Have each student choose any sixteen words from the word wall and write one word per square. Now that children have their word grids ready, call out a word from the word wall. Students who have that word on their papers can circle it. Continue to call out word wall words for students to circle on their papers. The first child to have all words circled "wins." Continue calling out words until everyone has all words circled.

Fold in half   Fold in half again.   Fold again   Fold again   unfold

Write a Sentence

Each child writes a sentence using as many word wall words as possible.
Then, they underline the word wall words with their favorite color crayons.
Children can take turns reading sentences aloud and classmates can identify the word wall words.

Word Shapes

This activity works with a word wall of high-frequency words that have word shapes outlined. Draw word shapes for five word wall words on the chalkboard. Students number their papers and write the words. Have children share their answers. There may be more than one correct word for some word shapes.

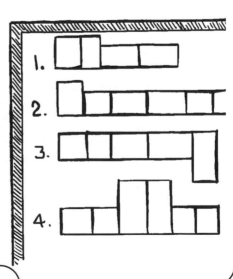

Practice & **LearnRight**

Perfect Score Spelling Test

This spelling test encourages successful learning experiences for every child in the class. It is a word wall spelling test where everyone can get a perfect score. Say the word. Students find the word on the word wall and copy it. Check papers together. This activity helps children locate words on the word wall and helps them remember which words are on the wall. After the test, tell children to use their favorite color crayon to put a star or a big happy face on their papers. Celebrate success!

Thinking Hats

Kids have to put on their "thinking hats" for this "test." Say, "Write the word that begins with s and rhymes with much. Continue giving rhyming words, synonyms or antonyms for words on the word wall. This thinking activity sharpens word skills and challenges students.

Super Study Strips

Super Study Strips are used for writing word wall words. Use the reproducible on page 43 to make Super Study Strips. Cut each page into three strips and affix one to each student's desk. When you introduce a new word for the word wall, students write the new word on the desktop study strip. When ten words have been introduced, the study strip will be complete. Then children can take it home and show parents the ten latest words that have been added to the word wall at school.

The Super Study Strips are a desktop list for each student for the newest words on the word wall. Give a touch spelling test:

> Say the word.
> Have children point at the word.
> Then spell the word aloud together
> as students touch the letters with
> their fingertips.

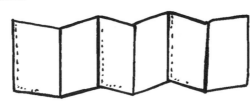

Fold Up Word Books

Fold up word books come in handy. Children can write a word on each page and take the little books home to study. Have students fold a paper in half lengthwise. Now, accordian fold it to make a book.

Fold lengthwise

Your Own Names

Youngsters use very important words for this activity -- their own names. They write their first names vertically. Then, they write a word wall word for each letter. They can draw a happy face for letters in their names for which there are no word wall words.

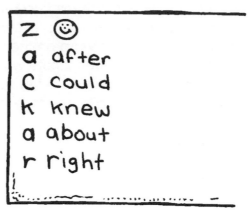

Dictation Sentences

This valuable activity clearly links listening, writing and reading. Give dictation sentences that include word wall words. Tell students to use the word wall for help spelling words. When you do dictation activities use the listen-say it-write it approach.

   Tell students to listen to the sentence.

   Then have the class repeat the sentence aloud with you.

   The children write the sentence as you repeat it again.

   Now, have everyone read the sentence aloud together.

When children hear the sentence and then say it aloud themselves, it is easier for them to remember the sentence and to write it down.

I'm Done List of Word Wall Activities

Every teacher has heard the words, "I'm done!" Your word wall is a source of activities for students to do when they finish early. Simply post a list on the chalkboard or on a chart of activities students can do when they have extra time. If you just want a few activities to be choices for today, put a check on stick-on notes beside those activities. Continue adding activities to the list throughout the year. Be sure to do each activity one time with the whole class. Then children will know how to do it independently.

I'm Done Activities for Our Word Wall

(Choose an activity that has a ☑ .)

Look at the word wall word that is hardest for you to spell. Write it, then trace it with your fingertip.

☑ Build three words with magnetic letters.

Write a word. Cut it apart letter by letter. Mix up the letters. Now spell the word with the letters.

☑ Write words using different color crayons for each letter.

Chose a word. Write it adding one letter on each line.

> t
> th
> the
> them

☑ Read the word wall from a to z.

Read the word wall with a partner from z to a.

Instant Word Wall Activities for Word Families

These activities are specific to word families. Most of the other activities in this book can also be used with word families.

Students Call Out
Write a rime on the chalkboard. Have students call out word family words to list on the chalkboard. As you write each word, underline the rime. When the list is complete, read it aloud with the class. For fun, do Stand-up and Sit-Down Reading described on page 25.

Cluster of Words
Write a rime in a circle on the chalkboard. Have students call out word family words for the rime. Instead of listing words, make a cluster of words around the rime in the center. After doing this activity as a whole class, students can do clusters individually or with partners for other rimes.

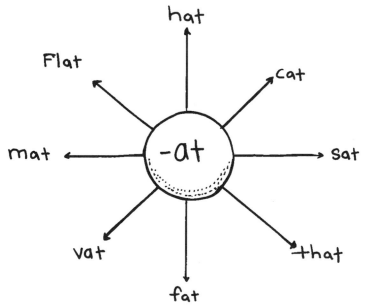

Three Minutes
Write a rime on the chalkboard. Give the class three minutes to write as many word family words as they can. Then list words on the chalkboard.

Thinking Aloud

Teach strategies by thinking aloud and modeling for your class. It's easy and it's effective! During classroom reading and writing activities, teachers should model decoding by analogy using the word wall. Be sure to refer frequently to the word wall for help reading and spelling words.

For example:

"Are there any words on the word wall that can help us spell flashlight? Mmmm, let's see. Here's the word dash...that can help us spell flash...and here's the word night...that can help us spell light. "

Adding Machine Paper

Expand word skills in a fun way -- give each student a strip of adding machine paper. Have children write a rime on top and then list the word family words for the rime. Have students underline the rime in each word family word.

Read and Learn Cards

Read and Learn Cards help students become experts at reading word family words. Cut cards that are 9 x 12 cards from oak tag. Or, cut file folders in half. You need 37 or 38 cards. Write a common rime at the top of the card and list word family words below on the card. Students can use the cards to practice reading word family words. Make a card for each of the thirty-seven common rimes. Use the thirty-seven rimes listed on page 17. From these rimes students can make over five hundred words.

Word Family Cards

When your class brainstorms word family words write the list on the chalkboard. Make word cards for each word in the word family and place cards in an envelope. Do this each time you introduce a new word family. Eventually you will have an envelope for each of the thirty-seven common rimes. These word family cards are valuable for practicing word family words and for word sorting activities.

Sort Word Families
Mix up two or more sets of cards. Give the cards to pairs of small groups of students to sort according to word families.

Word Family Spelling Test
Give a word family spelling test. Have children divide their papers into three columns. Write three rimes on the chalkboard that you want them to write at the tops of the columns. Then say a word family word. Children must write the word in the column under the word famliy rime.

-at	-op	-ug

Guessing Games
Children love guessing games. This game involves some guessing and a lot of thinking. Place a word card for a word wall word in an envelope. Pull it out so students can see the first letter. Tell them how many letters are in the word. Reveal another letter and ask students to look at the word wall and write down what the word might be. Then reveal another letter. Continue to do this until the word is known.

Practice & **LearnRight**

Word Family Cubes

Use empty square tissue boxes for cubes.
Paste light color construction paper
squares on the sides of the cubes.

Rime Cubes

Cubes are fun to roll and make learning activities exciting.
Use seven cubes for this activity. Write the thirty-seven rimes
on construction paper squares and paste on the sides of cubes.
Since there are forty-two sides and only thirty-seven common rimes, simply repeat
five of the rimes so you have a rime on the side of each cube. Roll the cubes one at
a time and have the class call out words in the word families.

Family Cubes

Expand word skills in a fun way! Make a cube for each word family. Write a rime on
each cube. Then elicit words in the word family to print on the cube. Do this for each
of the thirty-seven common rimes. Place the cubes in a reading center where students can practice reading the words on the cubes.

You can make individual cubes with the reproducible cube on page 42.

Word Families Bulletin Boards

Educate and decorate with these bulletin board ideas that focus on word families.

Word Families Trains Bulletin Boards
Use the pattern to cut 37 locomotives. Write a rime on each one and post on a bulletin board. When you work on a word family, write word family words on cars for the train cut from light-colored construction paper.

It's a good idea to use one color for all the cars on a word family train. Then use a different color for the cards on the next train. This makes the word families stand out on the bulletin board.

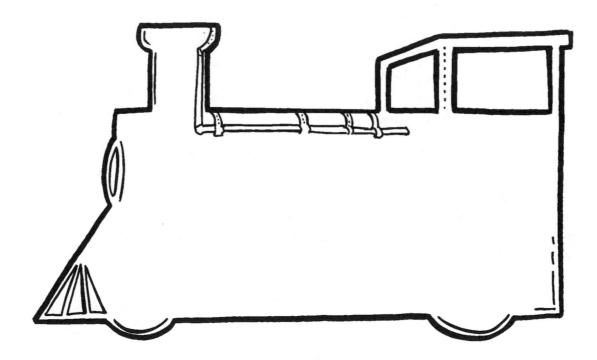

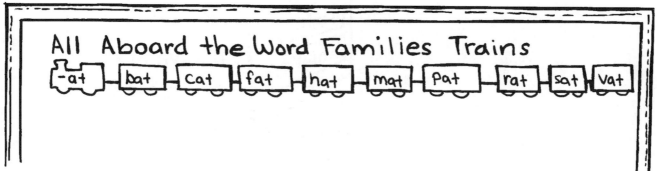

Practice & **LearnRight**

Kids like critters, kites and ice cream. Capitalize on these themes for word families bulletin boards to brighten your classroom. Make a critter, kite or ice cream cone for each of the thirty-seven common rimes. Each time you work on a new word family, add it to the bulletin board.

Creepy Crawley Critters Bulletin Board

High-flying Word Families

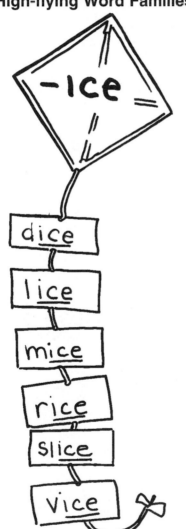

Super Scoops of Word Families

Practice & **LearnRight**

39

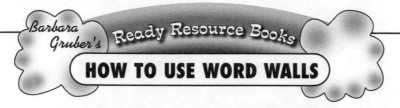

Word Skills Learning Station

Pick a spot in the classroom on a table or countertop where you can place materials that go with word skills and your word wall. Look at this list of materials you may want to include at the word skills center:

- Paper and pencils

- Magnetic letters

- Rubber alphabet stamps

- Word Wall Jingles Cards - page 14

- Rings of Word Wall Words and a timer - page 22

- Speedy Reader Challenge Cards - page 27

- Blank Mini-Word Cards - page 28

- Desktop Word Walls - page 28

- Read and Learn Cards for Word Families - page 35

- Word Families Envelopes - page 36

- Word Cubes - page 37

Practice & **LearnRight**

Ready-to-Reproduce Pages for Word Wall Activities

Word Cubes (page 42)
Write six words on the cube and then reproduce a copy for each student. Or, reproduce the cube pattern for each student and have students write words on the sides of the cube.

Super Study Strips (page 43)
Run study strips off before writing words. Cut into thirds and give each student a strip. Study strips can be taped to students' desks. When you introduce new words students write them on study strips. Strips can be taped to students' desktops. Or, write words on the strips before reproducing them. Give word lists to students to use at school or home.

Awards (page 44)
Give children a pat on the back for learning their words!

Pop Corn (page 45)
Dog Bones (page 46)
Reproduce and have children write words on the worksheets. Perfect for word families!

Practice Makes Perfect! (page 47)
This take-me-home reproducible helps children practice words effectively. And, they can add the words they need to practice!

Word Cube Pattern

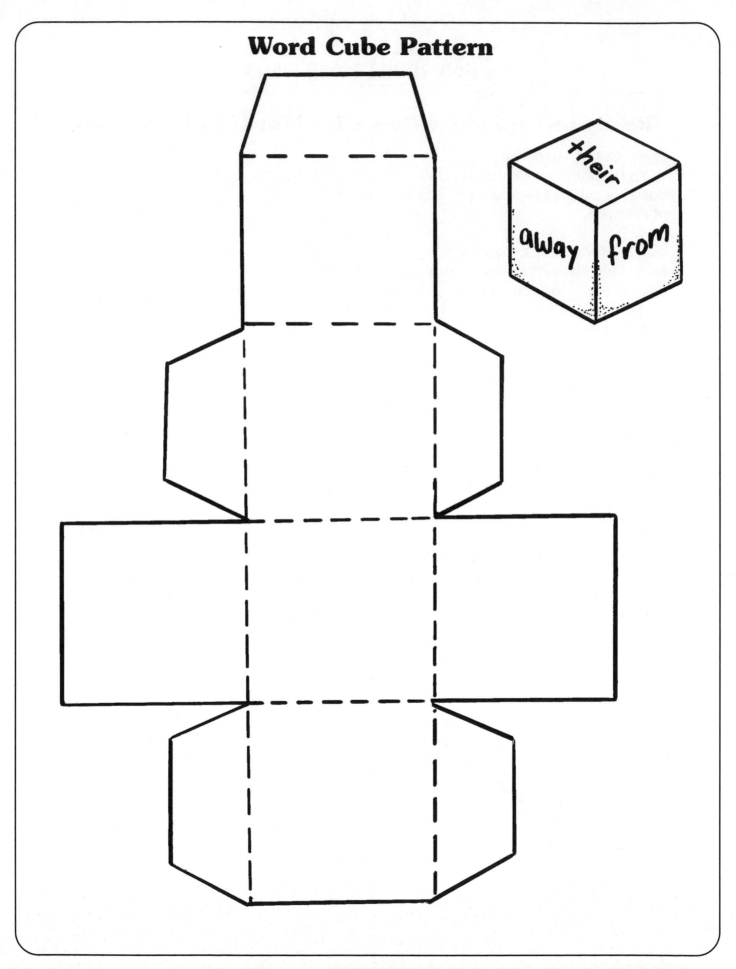

reproducible

Words to Learn		Words to Learn		Words to Learn
1		1		1
2		2		2
3		3		3
4		4		4
5		5		5
6		6		6
7		7		7
8		8		8
9		9		9
10		10		10

I can
read a
bunch of
words!

_____
Name

_____
Teacher

All Star Reader

_____
Name

_____
Teacher

_____
Name

can read the
word wall words!

_____
Teacher

Outstanding
Reader Award

_____
Name

_____
Date

44

reproducible

Name_____

1.

2.

3.

Popcorn

4.

5.

6.

7.

8.

9.

10.

11.

12.

Name _____

1.

2.

3.

4.

5.

6.

7.

8.

9.

10.

reproducible

Practice Makes Perfect

How to practice your words-

1. Look at the word.
2. Say the word.
3. Spell it.
4. Picture it.
5. Write it.

I will Practice these words!

_____   _____

_____   _____

_____   _____

_____   _____

_____   _____

_____   _____

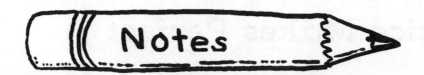